VOLVO BUSES AND COACHES

Howard Berry

AMBERLEY

First published 2020

Amberley Publishing
The Hill, Stroud
Gloucestershire, GL5 4EP

www.amberley-books.com

British Library Cataloguing in Publication Data.
A catalogue record for this book is available from the British Library.

ISBN 978 1 4456 7608 1 (print)
ISBN 978-1-4456-7609-8 (ebook)

Typesetting and Origination by Amberley Publishing.
Printed in Great Britain.

Introduction

The origins of Volvo (Latin for 'I roll') go back to 1911 when the name was registered as a trademark by Swedish company Svenska Kullagerfabriken (or SKF, as it is better known) for a proposed new series of ball bearings. The idea was shelved, and SKF used its own initials for all its ball bearing products. Nothing more was heard of Volvo until 1924, when Assar Gabrielsson, one of SKF's sales managers, and engineer Gustav Larson decided to construct a car that could withstand the rigours of Sweden's rough roads and cold temperatures. AB Volvo was formed in 1926 and a year later the firm commenced manufacturing cars as a subsidiary of the SKF group using the production line at the factory in Hisingen in Gothenburg. The first Volvo bus, the B1, was launched in 1934, by which time Volvo had already commenced exporting lorries to Europe.

In 1964, Volvo loaned an L4751 lorry to a London haulier, and this came to the attention of Jim McKelvie, a prominent Scottish haulier. Noting that unlike lorry manufacturers from other countries, UK companies such as Leyland and ERF were failing to keep up with the developments in such fields as engineering, performance and driver comfort, he commenced an in-depth study of the truck manufacturing industry, ending up with only Scania and Volvo as suitable candidates for a proposed business venture. One of his friends was Jim Keyden, former Managing Director of the Pressed Steel factory in Linwood where the shells for the Volvo P1800 car were built. McKelvie's company would then take the shells by road to the Jensen factory in West Bromwich, where they were mated with mechanical components delivered from Sweden. After Keyden told McKelvie how high Volvo's engineering standards were, his decision was made and he persuaded Volvo to sell him some F86 lorries to test the UK market, and in 1967 both men joined forces to form Ailsa Trucks Ltd, the sole UK importer of Volvo trucks. Based in Barrhead, 9 miles south-west of Glasgow, the company name was taken from Ailsa Craig, a rocky outcrop in the Firth of Clyde just off the south Ayrshire coast. The company grew rapidly because of the success of the Volvo F86 and the aftercare received from Ailsa Trucks. Now with a foothold in the UK lorry market, Volvo was keen to break into the UK bus and coach market. In 1971, in order to handle the proposed sales, spare parts and servicing of buses and coaches in the UK and Republic of Ireland, Ailsa Bus Ltd was set up as a wholly owned subsidiary of Ailsa Trucks Ltd, with McKelvie and Keyden as sole directors.

Throughout the decades that followed, sales of Volvo vehicles continued to climb steadily, with Volvo claiming record market shares in certain sectors. In 1978, Ailsa Trucks Ltd changed its name to Volvo Trucks (Great Britain) Ltd, with Ailsa Bus becoming Volvo Bus (Great Britain) Ltd the following year. In 1988, both sectors of the former Ailsa company were fully acquired by the Volvo Bus Corporation. The same year it acquired its biggest competitor in the UK PSV market – Leyland. In 1986, the UK Government was wishing to divest itself of the state-owned British Leyland, or Rover Group as it was now known, and so split it into separate manufacturing divisions, the PSV sector becoming Leyland Bus and sold to a management buyout team. Two years later in March 1988, Volvo Bus Corporation purchased Leyland Bus and, with Ailsa Bus Ltd never formally wound up but remaining a dormant company, it was revived and renamed VL Bus & Coach UK, bringing Volvo Bus (UK) Ltd and Leyland Bus together, resulting in those long-time rivals the Volvo B10M and Leyland Tiger being marketed by one company. It also highlighted manufacturing overcapacity, resulting in closure of the former Leyland plants at Faringdon and Workington, as well as a reduction in the vehicles within the Leyland range. As a result, in 1993 the Leyland name disappeared from UK bus manufacturing altogether, leaving Volvo as the market leader for PSV chassis in the UK.

My association with Volvo coaches goes back over thirty-five years, when I sat behind the wheel of KAF 129W, the first 'foreign' coach of Roselyn Coaches. Compared to the rest of the fleet, which was made up of AEC, Bedford, Ford and Seddon, it seemed a world apart, with what appeared to be air-assisted everything, and a dashboard with more lights than a Christmas tree. Since then I have always been an admirer of the marque, and having racked up many tens of thousands of miles behind the wheel without as much as a failure, I was always confident that, when driving a Volvo, I would indeed roll. With so many different Volvo models on the market today, but only 96 pages available, and with little interest in the faceless almost silent buses of today, I have restricted the timescale in this book to the first forty years of Volvo in the UK, an era that I feel confident and competent to talk about within the (hopefully) informative and sometimes humorous captions. As with my previous publications I have been greatly assisted in my endeavours by a handful of photographers to whom I am indebted, not only for letting me use their work but also for having the foresight to record these vehicles in their heyday for others to enjoy so many years later. Each photographer has an initialled credit after their work – these are Alan Snatt (AS), Martyn Hearson (MH), Richard Simons (RS) and Paul Green (PG). Finally, talking of initials, within the photo captions, NBC refers to the National Bus Company, and SBG to the Scottish Bus Group.

The 1970s – A Star Is Born

Volvo shipped the first right-hand drive passenger chassis to the UK in 1970, where it stood in Ailsa's yard for eighteen months before being sent to Walter Alexander in Falkirk to be fitted with an Alexander 'Y' type body. In 1971, buoyed by the success of lorry sales, Ailsa Trucks set up a stand-alone subsidiary, Ailsa Bus Ltd, not only to provide sales and service backup for the forthcoming PSV range, but to design and build products of its own at Barrhead. Knowing the SBG's aversion to rear-engined buses, Ailsa Bus realised that Volvo's 6.7-litre TD70 engine was compact enough to fit a front-engined double-decker with the entrance ahead of the front axle. Ailsa worked closely with both the SBG and Alexander's to design such a vehicle, to be assembled in Scotland, with the aim of the SBG becoming a major purchaser. Jim McKelvie travelled to Gothenburg to present a case study on Ailsa Trucks Ltd assembling current models in the Volvo truck range, and Ailsa Bus Ltd manufacturing the new double-deck bus. Not only was approval given, but Volvo also purchased a 75 per cent stake in Ailsa and, realising that the Barrhead site was not big enough for the new venture, gave approval for the lease of a 70-acre former Royal Ordnance depot in Irvine, with the site being purchased outright in 1973.

It was hoped the new chassis (which had been given the Volvo designation code B55) would be ready for the 1972 Earls Court Motor Show, however it was not to be. This didn't prevent Ailsa from putting on a major display. On show were examples of the B58 and B59, both 11 metres long and fitted with Volvo's 9.6-litre THD100 engine. The B59 had the engine at the rear, could be mated to SCG semi-automatic or Voith fully automatic gearboxes and had air suspension as standard. At the show, as well as a demonstration chassis, one complete vehicle was on display, VEB 566L, fitted with a light and airy Marshall Camair body. Despite being well received and spending time with operators across the country, it was to be the only B59 built to UK specification. Several factors were against it – firstly, it was too expensive, the cheapest chassis and body combinations costing approximately £14,000. Secondly, it was simply ahead of its time. The major city corporations required high-capacity double-deckers, the NBC owned 50 per cent of the competing Leyland National, the SBG was averse to operating rear-engined buses, municipal operators only usually bought small numbers of single-deck buses, and at the time the independent sector was primarily concerned with coaching operations.

In complete contrast, the other show model became the UK's first successful imported PSV chassis. The B58 had its THD100 engine mounted amidships, and over its lifetime was available with semi-automatic, fully automatic or manual gearboxes. Early models were fitted with Volvo's own five- or six-speed all-synchromesh boxes before the more reliable ZF six-speed manual was made available, many having a distinctive 'kinked' gearstick designed for ease of access to the cab area. Fitted with an exhaust brake and power steering as standard, its specification was way above home market chassis such as AEC and Leyland. The show exhibit, LBW 185L, was fitted with a Plaxton Panorama Elite body and delivered to Heyfordian of Upper Heyford two months later, giving them the honour of being the UK's first Volvo coach operator. Others were quick to follow, and by the end of 1973 over forty B58s had entered service, including into high-profile fleets such as Skill's of Nottingham, Whippet of Fenstanton, and Park's of Hamilton.

By the time the B58 was succeeded by the B10M in 1982, nearly 1,500 had entered the UK market, the vast majority bodied as coaches.

The B55 project was advancing at pace, and a prototype was completed in 1973, with the model (which by now had been officially named the Ailsa) launched that November at the Scottish Motor Show. This coincided with the launch of the Scania/ MCW Metropolitan double-decker, and these two Swedish-based, British-built buses were hailed as the first of the new generation of double-deck buses designed specifically for driver-only operation. The original Ailsas had the TD70 engine coupled to a SCG semi-automatic gearbox, its lightweight and high-revving but economical engine endearing it to Scottish operators in particular, and the fact that most were bodied by Alexander's in Falkirk meant the majority of Ailsas were built entirely in Scotland, a significant factor in securing orders from the SBG, Strathclyde PTE and Tayside, the biggest home market Ailsa operator. In 1977, the improved MKII version appeared, available with Voith or Allison automatic or SCG pneumocyclic gearboxes and retarder. The MKIII version introduced in 1980 continued to use the TD70H turbocharged engine, but with the gearbox and fuel tanks moved rearwards to improve front end weight. The floor was lowered by 40 mm. In direct contrast to the B58, nearly all Ailsas were double-deckers, and after Strathclyde PTE converted an accident-damaged example to single-deck, they took delivery of NHS 782Y, bodied from new as a single-decker by Marshall's, the same company who bodied the solitary B59. It was an attempt to break into the sector dominated by more complicated rear-engined designs, but by now, even though the Ailsa was seen as a very cost-effective, competitively priced bus, its front engine layout was seen as old-fashioned, especially when competitors were offering models with full air suspension and more ergonomically friendly driving compartments, and the last home market Ailsas were delivered to Strathclyde PTE at the end of 1984.

Above and below: The start of it all... Alexander 'Y' type-bodied B58 BUS 653K was the first Volvo PSV in the UK. Delivered as a chassis to Ailsa Trucks in 1970, the choice of bodywork may seem surprising, but with supply to the SBG clearly in Ailsa's sights, having both body and chassis supplied by Scottish-based companies was seen as a positive selling point. It was eventually sold to Park's of Hamilton, but by 1984 had passed to Astons of Kempsey in Worcestershire, where the Alexander body was removed, the chassis lengthened, and a new Van Hool Alizee body fitted. It is seen with its final operator, Village Green Motor Services of Shobdon in Herefordshire, registered VIL 4057. (AS/MH).

Seen in the demonstration park at the 1972 Earls Court Commercial Motor Show is VEB 566L, the Marshall Camair-bodied B59. Despite its attractive appearance and a speed reputed to be so high that top gear had to be locked out, it remained unique in the UK. Just like the B58 demonstrator, it too passed to Park's of Hamilton when its demonstration days were over. (AS)

The first Ailsa built (chassis number 73001) was Alexander-bodied THS 273M. It spent the first years of its life on demonstration duties across the British Isles before joining the Hong Kong Citybus fleet as BZ 5769. In 1974 it spent some time on loan to South Yorkshire PTE and is seen here returning from Cantley on Service 170. (RS)

Golden Miller of Feltham was the first operator to place a multiple order for the B58, taking three Duple Dominant-bodied examples in early 1973. The first to arrive was MYV 792L, which was also the first Duple-bodied Volvo. It is seen at the 1972 British Coach Rally at Brighton with some rather spirited driving from the mark 1 Ford Escort behind. (AS)

One well-known name prepared to take a gamble with the new B58 chassis was Skill's of Nottingham, who ordered two Duple Dominant-bodied examples in 1973. FTV 10L is seen departing Doncaster's South bus station in a rather lively manner on one of Skill's day excursions to the Yorkshire coast. (RS)

In 1929, H.W. Hunter began running from Seaton Delaval to North Shields. The route overlapped the United Automobile service, and soon regular passengers waited for Hunter's rather than travel with United. Hunter's ceased trading in 1994, operating their stage-carriage service to the end. Twenty years earlier, they took one of the first B58s fitted with the Express version of Plaxton's Panorama Elite body, and 33 (PJR 157M) is seen in Northumberland Square, North Shields when new. (RS)

Another operator quick to put a Panorama Elite Express-bodied B58 onto service work was Premier (Harold Wilson) of Stainforth. RYG 169M stands at Doncaster Christ Church while operating the service to Moorends. (AS)

Douglas Park was evidently impressed by the Volvo demonstrators, as, since the first Volvo entered the Park's of Hamilton fleet, nearly 1,400 have been delivered. Wearing Park's all-black livery is Duple Dominant-bodied RVD 606M, one of six delivered in 1974. Seen travelling down Strand when new. (AS)

8002 KV was new in 1973 as NVD 725L, Park's of Hamilton's first Duple Dominant-bodied B58. Ten years later it passed to Happy Days of Woodseaves in Staffordshire where it received a new Plaxton Paramount 3200 body. Subsequently moving a couple of miles north to join the fleet of Graham's Coaches of Talke, it is seen just prior to entering service after being prepared to Graham's usual high standards. Rumours were rife that it felt unstable, with reports that its rear wheels sometimes lifted off the road when cornering! (MH)

R. I. Davies of Tredegar was one of the first operators to start going 'over the water' after proprietor Hilling Davies went abroad on honeymoon in 1962 and realised there was a market for continental coach holidays. The first tours ran a year later and became extremely popular, with continental destinations emblazoned down the side of the coaches, as seen on 1974 Panorama Elite Express-bodied B58 OWO 906M. With the death of Hilling Davies, OWO passed with most of the Davies fleet to Hill's of Tredegar. (RS)

Hill's purchased one of the earliest B58s, but maybe the marque failed to impress, as only six more were purchased on top of the ones taken over with the Davies fleet. Seen at the back of Sophia Gardens in Cardiff is Plaxton Elite Express HUH 769N, new in 1975. (RS)

In 1986, HUH 769N's chassis was sent to Plaxton to be fitted with a new Paramount 3200 body and remained in the fleet until the end of Hill's operations in 1991. When it first arrived in Tredegar it was re-registered HFH 202 (Harry Hill being the managing director), later becoming DSU 751, the plate it retained when seen with Whiteheads of Conisbrough in 1994. (RS)

Seen in Weston-super-Mare, Van Hool-bodied JVW 426N was the first production B58 fitted with a body other than by Plaxton or Duple and was delivered to Harris of Grays in 1975. No one would have guessed at the time that within twenty years, the Van Hool/Volvo combination would go on to become the most popular in the UK. (RS)

In my humble opinion, one of the most graceful bodies was the Alexander 'M' type, built specifically for the SBG's overnight Scotland to London services, and fitted with rear-mounted toilets (long before such a luxury became commonplace) and oil-fired heating. With seats for only forty-two passengers, XV2540 (HSD 711N) was new to Western Scottish in 1975 and is seen entering London Victoria coach station at the end of its long journey from the north. (AS)

When its period of nocturnal running was over, sister ship HSD 710N passed to Stevensons of Uttoxeter who removed the toilet and replaced the outward swinging coach door with a conventional one. It is seen here in Derby bus station with other members of Stevensons eclectic fleet in the background. (RS)

Despite their arduous working lives, the Alexander-bodied B58s were surprisingly long-lived. After sale by Western SMT, the former XV2537 (HSD 708N) passed to Parkinson & Gordon, Leeds (Four Seasons) where it was re-registered BYC 696B. It is seen entering Wembley Stadium when nearly sixteen years old, and again has received a conventional door conversion. (AS)

In 1975, Greater Glasgow PTE took delivery of fifteen Ailsas fitted with curvy, panoramic Alexander bodies more usually associated with the fleet's Leyland Atlanteans. They remained unique, all subsequent deliveries having the 'boxy' bodywork fitted to the majority of Ailsas. MGE 183P was fleet number AV8, and subsequently passed to Black Prince of Morley, where it is seen on New Market Street in Leeds. Happily, this significant vehicle has been preserved. (RS)

In 1971, Van Hool took over the Dublin bodybuilding factory of Irish National Transport Company (CIE), and joined forces with Dundalk-based coachbuilders Thomas McArdle to form Van Hool-McArdle. It built sixty-four bodies on the Ailsa, sixty-two of which were delivered to South Yorkshire PTE. 374 (LWB 374P) was the only one to receive the South Yorkshire Transport livery, this being the arm's length company set up by the PTE to operate buses across South Yorkshire in preparation for deregulation. (RS)

In 1987, thirteen of the SYPTE Ailsas were sold to London Buses, where twelve were allocated to Potters Bar garage to undertake Hertfordshire County Council contract services, the thirteenth being used for spares. Seen resplendent in red London Buses livery but devoid of any fleet name is V13 (LWB 369P). (AS)

In 1974, West Midlands PTE took delivery of three Alexander-bodied Ailsas, and so became the first operator to put an Ailsa into service. They were followed two years later by a further fifty, but with the MCW Metrobus being built at Washwood Heath, it was considered more politically correct to buy the local product, and so no further Ailsas were ordered. Alexander-bodied 4760 (JOV 760P) is seen in Paradise Circus, Birmingham. (AS)

In 1987, all the 1976 delivered West Midlands Ailsas were sold to London Buses. Some joined the ex-SYPTE ones at Potters Bar, others going to Harrow Weald depot for the low-cost tendered unit of Harrow Buses. Those allocated to Potters Bar looked stunning in their London Buses red with black skirt as seen on V57 (JOV 757P) passing the wonderfully named Bat & Goldfish in Barnet. (AS)

The only low-height Ailsa was Derby Borough Transport's Alexander-bodied 71 (RTO 1R). In January 1976, shortly after Derby acquired Blue Bus Service of Willington, a fire at the former Blue Bus garage destroyed most of the vehicle allocation. Blue Bus required low-height deckers owing to a low bridge in Willington village, and RTO 71R arrived in 1977 to replace vehicles hired from other fleets. The difference in upper and lower deck window heights can be clearly seen. (RS)

The NBC's only Ailsas (as well as its first Volvos) were five with Alexander bodies delivered to Maidstone & District in 1976. They were part of a one-year trial alongside five Scania/MCW Metropolitans and four Bristol VRs. Detailed reports on fuel and oil consumption, maintenance work and comments by drivers and garage staff were made. Despite the Ailsas receiving favourable comments, the British Leyland-owned Bristol VR became the NBC's standard double-decker. The large fleet number on the front dome of LKP 382P was to make identification easier on the CCTV in Chatham's Pentagon bus station. (MH)

As well as buying one of the first B58s, Harold Wilson (Premier) of Stainforth were the only English independent to buy a new Ailsa, taking Alexander-bodied NET 520R in 1976. It was hired to operate a trip over the Humber Bridge on the day of its opening and is seen here stuck in traffic on the A15 at the Barton-on-Humber side approach to the bridge. (RS)

Introduced into the UK market in 1969, Portuguese-built Caetano bodywork rapidly established itself on the coaching scene. They were imported by Loughborough-based dealer Alf Moseley and marketed under the Moseley Continental name, hence the AM initials in the front panel and 'Moseley Continental' badge behind the front door. The Lisboa was fitted to heavyweight chassis as seen here on Monty Moreton of Nuneaton's B58 UDU 368R, one of three new in 1977 when coaches of entirely foreign manufacture were still a novelty in British coach parks. (RS)

Years ago I was asked to go to a local coach dealer, hand over a cheque and collect the keys to a 'new' coach. I should have asked the operator in question to define new, as I came away with twenty-five-year-old Plaxton Viewmaster-bodied TGD 995R. New to Park's, it subsequently passed to Webber's of Blisland in Cornwall, whose livery it carried when collected, and remained in during its time with said operator. Seen here while with Webber's, it is parked in Exeter services on the M5. (PG)

The two Van Hool McArdle-bodied Ailsas not delivered to SYPTE went to J. Hunter of Ardrossan, a member of Ayrshire Bus Owners (A1 Service) Ltd, a co-operative based around Ardrossan, Kilmarnock and Irvine. With the Ailsa manufactured 'just down the road', it was fitting that A1 Service members purchased a further ten examples. Arriving in Kilmarnock with the town's viaduct as an impressive backdrop, PSJ 825R is sandwiched between products of the British Leyland Group, a Mastiff tractor unit to the right and Marina van to the rear. (MH)

It wasn't until January 1978, twelve months after the penultimate delivery, that SHL 930S, SYPTE's final Ailsa, entered service. It was originally a standard Mk 1 Ailsa and was bodied alongside the rest of the batch, however during shipping the body was seriously damaged. The opportunity was taken use the chassis as the prototype Mk II, and it was fitted with a Voith gearbox. In 1986 it was withdrawn from service and converted for use as SYPTE's roadshow bus. (RS)

In 1978, Cardiff borrowed a brand-new Alexander-bodied Ailsa from Tayside for evaluation, with Cardiff sending a Willowbrook-bodied Bristol VR up to Dundee in return. Tayside remained loyal to the Ailsa, but Cardiff became a convert, purchasing thirty-six fitted with Northern Counties bodywork. With bodyside advertising promoting holidays in Tayside, SSN 247S is seen on layover in Cardiff bus station. (RS)

Edinburgh St Andrews bus station sees two standard Eastern Scottish vehicles, but one non-standard livery. Parked next to Plaxton Supreme IV-bodied Seddon LCS 956T is Alexander-bodied Ailsa VV773 (CSG 773S) wearing an overall advertisement for the SBG's Edinburgh to London service. How times have changed – the price of a single fare in 1980 was a mere £7.50. (MH)

Len Wright of Isleworth became synonymous with continental shuttle work, as well as the transportation of rock and pop groups on worldwide tours, and made Volvo the chassis of choice for their high-specification coaches. New in 1977, B58 FAA 757S was the first to be delivered, its Plaxton Supreme body containing only forty seats with tables, toilet, and full catering servery. (RS)

The only double-deck B58 was KBT 343S, new to Steve Stockdale of Selby in 1978 fitted with a Caetano Lisboa body. It passed to Skill's of Nottingham, where following an accident in 1992 it was fitted with a semi-automatic gearbox and sent to East Lancs for rebodying. Found to be very light at the rear, it was returned to East Lancs on a number of occasions to have weights (paving stones encased in steel angle sections to retain them in place) fitted, which made it sluggish due to being too heavy. Skill's decided not to accept it and it was eventually sold to Reliance of Great Gonerby for their Grantham to Nottingham service, and remained as KBT 343S throughout its existence. (RS)

Well there's no doubting what this is... with the exception of a solitary Mercedes-Benz delivered in 1971, Wallace Arnold ordered nothing other than British-built chassis, primarily Fords and Leyland Leopards until 1978 when four Plaxton Supreme-bodied B58s entered the Leeds fleet. It was to be the beginning of the end for the British stronghold, as in a few short years Volvo became the standard chassis supplier. The first of the four was XWX 198S, seen at Fairfield Halls, Croydon when brand new. (AS)

The other big coup for Volvo was infiltrating that other staunch buyer of British-built vehicles – Smiths Happiway-Spencers. Like Wallace Arnold, they too ran Fords, but preferred the AEC Reliance as their heavyweight chassis. The first of what was to become their standard chassis supplier entered the fleet in 1979, a batch of six Duple Dominant II-bodied B58s, and BTB 714T is seen arriving at Wembley in 1984. (AS)

Despite Heyfordian buying the first B58 delivered to a UK operator, it was not until 1979 that they purchased any further new Volvos. A substantial investment for the Oxfordshire company saw ten Van Hool Aragon-bodied B58s enter the fleet, with several being delivered in Global Tours livery. As was popular in the early 1990s, they all received dateless registrations, with TUD 521T becoming 1435 VZ. It is seen in Headington in 1993. (PG)

Plaxton's Viewmaster was essentially a Supreme with additional height, and with additional height came additional weight. The first Viewmasters were fitted to Leyland Leopard chassis, the extra weight causing the Leopard to struggle when fully laden, but when fitted to the B58 it was a different kettle of fish. Wearing Blue Crest Holidays livery, Lea Valley Coaches of Bishop's Stortford took delivery of GWC 33T in 1979. (AS)

While the B58 was more suited for use as a premium coach chassis, some operators did specify it for fitting under bus bodies. The first to do so was Longstaff of Mirfield, who took delivery of Duple Dominant bus-bodied YHD 599V in 1979. It subsequently passed to Thornes of Hemingbrough in 1996 and was re-registered as BBT 380V. (AS)

A vehicle that was new to Thornes (or rather the associated fleet of Independent of Horsforth) was Plaxton Supreme IV-bodied B58 SMV 24. New in 1979 as FNW 24T, by the time this photograph was taken in York running the city centre shuttle between the Barbican and the Railway Museum, it had been modernised with the fitment of a Viewmaster windscreen. (RS)

Greater Manchester PTE was a tough nut to crack for manufacturers outside the British Leyland empire as GMPTE had standardised on the Leyland Atlantean and Daimler Fleetline for many years. At the end of the 1970s, alternative chassis started to enter the fleet, notably the MCW Metrobus. Seeing an opportunity, Volvo had Ailsa NNA 134W bodied by Northern Counties, GMPTE's preferred bodybuilder. It was to remain unique in the fleet and is seen prior to delivery in the demonstration park at the Birmingham Commercial Motor Show. Behind is another sign of the times: a new Volvo for Smiths Happiway-Spencers. (MH)

In 1980, to find a suitable replacement for its fleet of leased AEC Reliances, London & Country took two Duple Dominant-bodied B58s to be evaluated against a pair of Leyland Leopards. All were put to work primarily on the northern orbital Green Line route 734. Unfortunately for Volvo, the Leopards won the day and no more were ordered. DV2 (GPH 2V) is seen departing Addlestone for Woking when new. (AS)

Despite carrying the badge from an early Volvo F10 truck, the chassis under West Wales of Tycroes Plaxton Supreme-bodied 83 (BWN 811V) is definitely a B58, identified by the narrow rear axle track, clearly visible with the wheels inset within the bodywork. It is seen departing Bristol duplicating the 650 Swansea to London service when new. (RS)

Before Hounslow-based Travellers Coach Company operated their own vehicles, coaches were contracted in to carry out their tourist charter work. The first of literally hundreds of Van Hool-bodied Volvos to join the Park's of Hamilton fleet were ordered to carry out such work and were a pair of Van Hool Aragon-bodied B58s delivered in 1980. The second of the pair, LYS 867V shows no sign of its owner's identity as it sits at King's Cross. (AS)

The aptly named Birmingham firm of Flights operated a network of services between the West Midlands and London's airports under the 'Flightlink' banner. The services were registered as stage carriage, and so Flights were able to take advantage of the Bus Grant scheme, whereby the government paid a percentage of the purchase price of a new vehicle provided it spent a certain amount of time on stage-carriage work. Plaxton Viewmaster-bodied B58 GOP 710W is seen departing Heathrow for Birmingham in 1982. (AS)

A good comparison of British and Continental-built bodies from the same year is seen on a pair of B58s from the fleet of independent operator South Yorkshire Road Transport. KWT 616V, on the left, is fitted with a Van Hool Aragon, while sister KWT 617V has Plaxton Supreme IV Express coachwork. Both were new in 1980. (RS)

British Coachways was a consortium of independent coach operators spread across the UK, intended as serious competition to the then state-owned National Express and SBG on inter-city routes. From an initial six members in October 1982, over its two short years of operation it expanded to ten companies. Morris Bros of Swansea was one of the founding six and seen parked in Blackpool is Plaxton Supreme IV-bodied B58 FTH 990W, one of the few coaches to be painted into British Coachways livery. (RS)

As mentioned earlier, with the demise of the AEC Reliance, the Blundell Group, owners of Smiths Happiway-Spencer, made Volvo their standard chassis. In 1982, just prior to the introduction of the B10M they ordered thirty Duple Dominant IV-bodied B58s, three of which are seen parked in Eastbourne's Princes Park coach park in 1984. (AS)

One of the biggest rise and fall stories of the late 1970s/early 1980s was Trathen's. Originally from Yelverton on the edge of Dartmoor, they ran one of the first executive-style inter-city express coach services in the UK. They became one of the big players in the continental shuttle market, with bases in London as well as L'Orange in the south of France, but in 1985 they succumbed to financial failure. Van Hool Alizee-bodied NFJ 380W was one of their first B10Ms and is seen surrounded by fleetmates in Gloucester Road coach station, London. (AS)

Having purchased the unique low-height Ailsa in 1977, it was not until five years later that Derby purchased more, taking fifteen in 1982, two bodied by Marshall, the remainder like 109 (SRC 109X) bodied by Northern Counties. With a Greater Manchester PTE bus about to overtake it, the assumption would be that one vehicle was on loan to the other operator – turns out that the location is actually Westgate, Rotherham, with both buses on loan to SYPTE. (RS)

The 1980s – Business Is Booming

Just like the 1970s, Volvo entered the 1980s with two new models for the UK market, and as before one was front-engined and one was underfloor. Despite being available since 1966, the vertically mounted front-engined B57 didn't arrive in the UK until 1980. Being lighter than the B58, it was an attempt to crack the lightweight market currently monopolised by Bedford and Ford but, as seen with the Ailsa, operators were shying away from front-engined buses (as Ford was to find to its cost), and it came as no surprise that the B57 wasn't a success. Having a low chassis frame, the engine intruded into the saloon, and was therefore quite noisy, and only two were delivered to the UK. There is no denying that the B58 had been a success for Volvo, however its replacement went on to be the most popular chassis of its generation – the Volvo B10M. Fitted with full air suspension as standard and using the same 9.6-litre engine as the B58, the B10M was available in two power outputs: 242bhp and 276bhp. Standard gearbox was the ZF six-speed manual, with a splitter fitted to those vehicles with the 276bhp engine, while Allison semi-auto and SCG, Voith or ZF fully auto boxes were available as options. Volvo was happy to produce a top-of-the-range version of the B10M fitted with features to comply with Germany's Tempo 100 regulations (allowing coaches to travel at 100kph on autobahns) and when supplied in this specification the chassis came out at nearly £6,000 more than the B58. Volvo launched the B10M at the 1980 Geneva Motor Show, but strong orders for the B58 saw Volvo's UK division hold off introducing the model. By the middle of 1980, dealers were showing a reluctance to order B58s for stock, a consequence of a combination of positive reports on the B10M and Leyland talking about their replacement for the Leopard and AEC Reliance, and so it was decided to launch the B10M in the UK at the Birmingham Motor Show in October 1980. However, the B10M didn't replace the B58 overnight, and both models were available until all right-hand drive B58 chassis had been sold, appeasing operators who still wanted Volvo reliability without the added cost and features of the higher specification B10M. The B10M was available to the UK market in a wider variety of lengths and axle configurations than the B58, including an articulated version (B10MA) and a 12-metre-long tri-axle chassis (B10MT), and operators were quick to order double-deck coaches in this configuration for use on continental shuttle services where the additional luggage capacity came in very handy. In 1985, the management at Irvine identified a market for a 9-metre-long coach, however their colleagues in Sweden were unconvinced, saying the vehicle would look unbalanced. Not to be put off, Irvine sent a standard B10M chassis to Plaxton's, who had previous experience of cutting down coach chassis. The result pleased the Swedish board, and shortly afterwards the B9M entered mainstream production. Fitted with a downrated version of the THD100 engine, the 9 referred to its length, not engine capacity, and while the B9M name was used for marketing purposes, the official designation was the B10M-46, due to its 4,600-mm wheelbase.

In 1988 Volvo announced the B10M MkIII, hailed by Volvo as a bigger change than that from B58 to B10M, and the MkIII designation was widely used on vehicles and in publicity. Major changes were made to improve emissions and fuel efficiency and a new range of engines was introduced – the 262bhp THD102KA and the huge 340bhp THD102KD. Also announced was the newly developed G7 gearbox, fitted with Easy Gear Shift, which was a small car-sized gear-lever mounted on the side of the driver's seat. The driver still changed gear using the clutch pedal, but the change was controlled by microswitches. The system was designed to take the physical effort out of gear changes, as well as preventing mis-changes, thus improving clutch, engine and gearbox life as well as reducing driver fatigue. Some drivers (me included) loved the G7, but others struggled to get on with it and in later years, many B10Ms had their G7s replaced with a ZF manual box.

As mentioned in the previous chapter, the Ailsa was becoming outdated, and with the success of the B10M, the design team at Irvine began looking at using it as the Ailsa's replacement. They found that by lowering the chassis slightly, fitting low-profile tyres and moving one or two components, they could achieve a floor height to meet the legal requirement for a double-decker. With no mainstream bodybuilders prepared to take the project seriously, Marshall of Cambridge (who also bodied the sole B59 and single-deck Ailsa) were approached, and in April 1982 Strathclyde PTE took delivery of ESU 378X. Two months later, the Volvo board agreed that the new model, to be called the Citybus, was a viable proposition and the go-ahead was given for production to commence at Irvine, the factory being refurbished to allow for the new production line. The Citybus used a downrated version of the THD100 engine mated to SCG or ZF automatic gearboxes. Sales figures never matched those of the Ailsa (the two models being built side by side for two years). This was not because of the product itself, which in trials was found to be more economical than its rivals, but due to a declining double-deck bus market following deregulation of the bus industry, and the progressive reduction to the government's Bus Grant scheme. In 1987, the decision was made to transfer Citybus production to the main bus assembly plant in Boras, with the Citybus name being dropped. The chassis was then known as the D10M.

One final model from the Volvo catalogue available in the UK during the 1980s was completely different from anything offered before – the semi-integral C10M. Introduced in 1984, it used the THD101 engine producing 310bhp mounted centrally between the front and rear axle, providing better weight balance. Having no bodybuilding facilities of their own, Volvo contracted the work to Swiss coachbuilder Ramseier & Jenzer, who produced a 12-metre-long coach with a massive 7-metre wheelbase, reportedly to improve ride quality. The C10M was very highly equipped, with a remotely operated heating system, entertainment system with individual speakers for every seat, and a full catering servery as standard. Unfortunately, it cost 40 per cent more than the top specification B10M, and out of the eighty built, only ten were delivered to the UK. Production of the C10M ceased in 1986.

Duple's Goldliner was essentially a raised-height Dominant, with a standard Dominant front, leaving Goldliners not fitted with a destination box with an unusual stepped front end. Bywater of Rochdale's CNS 549X was new in 1981 and was Duple's Goldliner IV demonstrator. Fitted with only forty-four seats, the B10M is seen in Gloucester Road coach station, West London in 1982. (AS)

The trapezoid windows on the Goldliner III were intended to emulate the iconic American Greyhound coaches, however the thickness of the panels between the windows meant some passengers had almost no view at all. The SBG ordered several for Anglo-Scottish services, however Western Scottish B10M KV151 (TSD 151Y) was on a private hire when captured in Parliament Square, London. (AS)

Wallace Arnold were heavily involved in pre-production testing for the Leyland Tiger, however Leyland managed to spectacularly mishandle their 1981 coach order, and so ended a relationship going back over fifty years. As a result, the 1982 vehicle order was rather eclectic, with both Setra and Bova entering the fleet. The balance was made up of Plaxton-bodied B10Ms, and this combination featured heavily in the fleet for many years. Seen outside Columbus Ravine garage in Scarborough is Plaxton Supreme V-bodied 4120 WA, originally registered VWX 365X. (RS)

In the late 1970s, Wallace Arnold commenced operating services between the UK and Europe under the Euroways banner. Seen pulling into the waiting bays on Buckingham Palace Road is Euroways-liveried Plaxton Paramount 3500-bodied B10M FUA 384Y. The Paramount was introduced in 1983 as the Supreme's successor, and WA were one of the first operators of the type. (AS)

Cardiff became such enthusiastic Ailsa operators that as well as purchasing thirty-six new examples, they acquired second-hand vehicles from Merseybus and Fife Scottish, some arriving as late as 1999. 448 (DEM 822Y) was one of the ex-Merseybus vehicles and is seen on Wood Street approaching Cardiff bus station. (RS)

Delivered as part of London Transport's Alternative Vehicle Evaluation (AVE) trials, Ailsa V3 (A103 SUU) was a radical beast. As well as having its second door located at the rear rather than centre, it was fitted with two staircases to reduce dwell times by increasing passenger flow. Unfortunately, the second staircase created a blind spot at the rear door, meaning a conductor had to be carried. Subsequently rebuilt to single door but retaining both staircases, V3 is seen here after transfer to Potters Bar, travelling down Market Street in Enfield. (AS)

With the twin towers of the old Wembley Stadium decorated for Comic Relief day, Plymouth City Coach's Van Hool Alizee-bodied B10M MCO 658 arrives with a party of excited lads ready to watch the 1989 England vs Belgium Schoolboy International. MCO 658 was originally fitted to one of Plymouth's Metro-Cammell-bodied Leyland PD2s, while the B10M was new to Park's of Hamilton as A602 UGD. (AS)

Quirky Staffordshire operator Knotty Bus & Coach, operated by photo contributor MH, consisted principally of vehicles manufactured by AEC. However in 1989 a coach was needed urgently to carry the Grand Tahiti Ballet Company on a six-week tour starting and finishing in Paris. From a luggage point of view alone, nothing in the fleet was suitable, so a flying visit to Limebourne of London resulted in Berkhof Espirit-bodied B10M A674 THK being purchased. Then came a mad dash to Paris, followed by the first leg of the tour – a quick jaunt up to Aberdeen! (MH)

There was a time when the individualistic front-end styling identified a bus built for Nottingham City Transport. With the end of production of their favoured standards, the Daimler Fleetline and Leyland Atlantean, more modern designs were trialled. These included the Citybus, Leyland's mid-engined Lion, and two Dennis Falcon Vs fitted with rear-mounted Mercedes V6 engines. One of that pair can be seen behind East Lancs-bodied Citybus 399 (A399 CRA) with a Willowbrook-bodied Fleetline coming up behind. (MH)

The mid-1980s saw some NBC subsidiaries break away from the corporate standard of British-built chassis fitted with British-built bodywork, and some rather exotic designs arrived, including ten Jonckheere Jubilee P599-bodied B10Ms for National Travel (East). A307 XHE carries Club 18–30 Holidays livery for use on Mediterranean holiday shuttles. The Plaxton Supreme-bodied AEC Reliance of Yelloway seen in the background is quite fitting, as when NTE was acquired by ATL Holdings in 1987, A307 XHE was transferred across to the (by then) associated Yelloway fleet. (RS)

Six other B10Ms formed part of the 1983/4 NTE delivery and were possibly the most exotic NBC coaches of all. Still bodied by Jonckheere, but to the one-and-half-deck P90 design, the six coaches were classed as double-deck due to the fitment of a nine-seat lounge behind the rear axle. A317 XHE is seen arriving at VCS when brand new. (AS)

The SBG also had some B10Ms to a similar layout but this time fitted with Dutch-built Berkhof Emperor bodies. New in 1985, Western Scottish KV188 (B188 CGA) is seen about to pull onto the Glasgow stand, and as an indication as to how things were changing in the 1980s, the only other coach visible in VCS is also bodied by Berkhof. (AS)

Van Hool's rear lounge 'body on chassis' offering was the Astral, and seen here is B10MT KIG 2473, new as B377 PAJ to Martindale of Ferryhill. It spent nearly twenty years on shuttle runs before moving to Eccles to join my good mate Wesley's stunning Go Goodwin's fleet. Here it was converted into the ultimate corporate hospitality coach to assist with Goodwin's contract with the English Cricket Board, including full-length lifting rear end to allow the company's Bentley to be driven inside. Now who is that handsome driver…? (HB collection)

Another coach to receive a double-deck body was B10M A335 GFF, new in 1983 as Duple Caribbean-bodied A123 KCC. Rodger's of Weldon sent it to East Lancs for rebodying, and it returned with a new Pyoneer body. However however unlike the B58 on page 23, it retained its manual gearbox. It is seen in 2015 heading out for an afternoon school run from Oundle School. (PG)

For over thirty years, Bakers Dolphin of Weston-super-Mare operated a Weston–Bristol–London service under the London Flyer banner. Most Flyer passengers were going 'up the Smoke' for the day, so seating rather than luggage space was the priority. Wanting a double-deck coach with two full decks worth of seating, Bakers commissioned Van Hool to build 340 MYA (new as C342 GSD), the only full double-deck Van Hool B10M built. It was the tallest coach in the UK, the additional height being due to the lower-deck floor having to clear the mid-mounted engine. Seen in 1993, it is turning out of Park Lane at Marble Arch. (AS)

New to Hutchison of Overtown in 1984 as B947 ASU, A15 RBL was one of only two Van Hool 'Local Traffic' bodied B10Ms delivered to the UK. Essentially a low-height Alizee shell fitted with bus seats, destination gear and split entrance doors. Both passed to Rhondda Buses, hence the RBL registration plate, but when seen in Llandudno in 2003, it had moved north to operate for GHA Coaches of Wrexham. (MH)

It was unusual for municipal operators to purchase second-hand vehicles, especially from an independent operator, but Rossendale Transport did with East Lancs 'semi coach' bodied Citybus 33 (B183 FDM). New in 1985 to Wright's of Wrexham, a company who expanded massively following deregulation, like many others who became too big too quickly, it paid the ultimate price and closed in 1993. It passed to Rossendale with the closure of Wright's and is seen in Rossendale's depot in Rawtenstall. (RS)

Before becoming part of the mighty Arriva empire, Grey-Green was one of London's largest coach companies, operating a network of services from the capital to East Anglia and south-east England as well as a thriving private hire department. In 1985 they purchased sixteen Plaxton Paramount 3500-bodied B10Ms, all fitted with toilets, and B870 XYR is seen parked on Victoria embankment in London. (AS)

Above and below: In the 1990s, Grey-Green's operation moved more from coaching to bus work, and it made economic sense for redundant coaches to be rebodied as buses. East Lancs was chosen to take some of the 1985 Plaxton Paramount-bodied B10Ms for rebodying in 1992. Those fitted with single-deck bodies such as B860 XYR were visually acceptable, however those fitted with double-deck bodies had very short rear overhangs to compensate for the long wheelbase. The rather bizarre look can be seen on 163 (B863 XYR), advertising another part of the Cowie empire. (AS)

Despite the popularity of their coach bodies, Caetano only sold four of their 'Stagecoach' service bus bodies on full-size chassis. All fitted to B10Ms, Hutchison of Overtown received C982/3 KHS, and Golden Miller of Feltham C89 NNV and C188 RVV. There is no disputing the location, the twin towers of the original Wembley Stadium providing the backdrop as C89 NNV arrives in 1988. (AS)

Being a florist isn't an obvious way to enter the coach industry, but that's how Ralph Arrigoni started his business in the mid-1960s. Using an old coach to deliver flowers in West London when the Heathrow Sheraton hotel was being constructed, he successfully tendered for the job of running a courtesy coach between the hotel and Heathrow Airport. Ralph's Coaches eventually provided most of the airport car park and hotel shuttle coaches for many years. C852 EML was one of a batch of thirty-three-seat Plaxton Bustlers fitted to the B9M chassis. (AS)

The B9M name was purely for marketing purposes, the official designation being B10M-46, the 46 indicating the 4.6-metre wheelbase, clearly visible in Pulham's of Bourton-on-the-Water's Paramount 3200-bodied C193 CYO. The coach was one of the last delivered to Glenton of London and when new was fitted with only twenty seats, Glenton's coaches having reduced seating capacity to allow extra legroom for passenger comfort on their extended tours. (AS)

Looking like an Ailsa, Alexander-bodied C101 CUL was actually a London Transport experimental one-off, a Citybus with a Volvo Flygmotor Cumulo energy accumulator fitted between the gearbox and differential. When stopping, the accumulator collected kinetic energy, and released it during acceleration, reducing the engine load. LT leased it for three years, after which it was returned to Volvo, where the Cumulo system was replaced by a standard ZF gearbox. It soon passed to Black Prince of Morley and is seen here on The Headrow in Leeds. (AS)

Despite being an enthusiastic Ailsa operator, West Midlands PTE only ordered six further Volvos, all B10Ms fitted with rather angular Alexander 'P' type bodies. They were half of twelve experimental single-deck vehicles allocated to Wolverhampton for evaluation purposes in 1986, the other six being Leyland Lynxes, a model which went on to be their standard single-decker of the 1980s and 1990s. 1060 (C60 HOM) is seen in Wolverhampton bus station. (AS)

See what I mean about the individualistic front-end styling? Even when painted in the garish two-tone purple of fellow Nottingham operator Dunn-Line, Northern Counties-bodied Citybus C309 NRC is instantly recognisable as being ex-Nottingham City Transport. New in 1985, it is seen loading in Retford bus station for a trip to Tuxford. (RS)

Fife Scottish followed up its large Ailsa order with two batches of Citybuses, all bodied by Alexander and to a design broadly similar to the Ailsas. 914 (C794 USG) from 1986 is seen leaving Edinburgh on the Coastliner service to Leven, the 1987 reincarnation of a service originally started in 1964 as a joint venture between Fife and Eastern Scottish. (RS)

The first NBC bus operating subsidiary to be privatised was Badgerline, formerly Bristol Omnibus's countrybus division. Badgerline went on a Volvo buying spree, purchasing B10Ms including fourteen Van Hool Alizee-bodied coaches. They were delivered in a variety of liveries, including Roman City Holidays (D500 GHY) and National Express (D504 GHY), both parked in Battersea Wharf coach park. (AS)

With the advent of deregulation, Harris of Grays were quick to commence local bus operations under the imaginatively titled Harrisbus banner, and purchased four thirty-three-seat Plaxton Bustler-bodied B9Ms. D301 PEV is seen leaving Greys bus station, with the State Cinema in the background. Opened in 1938 and able to seat 2,200 people, its fully illuminated Compton organ rose from the orchestra pit on a lift and was used in the BBC production of *Lipstick on Your Collar*. (AS)

Above and below: Out of the ten Ramseier & Jenzer-bodied C10Ms delivered to UK operators, half went to that diehard Volvo operator Park's of Hamilton. New in 1986, C641 KDS initially passed to Albatross of Monkwearmouth, but subsequently passed to Viscount Central where it was registered XSU 907. Viscount Central was Burnley & Pendle's coach fleet, it being the trading name of Sandown of Padiham, a company acquired by Burnley & Pendle in 1986. The long wheelbase of the C10M is clearly evident. (RS/AS)

Seen picking up in Bradford Interchange, New Bharat Coaches of Southall's C10M D201 KWU was one of a pair new to Wallace Arnold in 1986. It is seen about to operate New Bharat's service from Bradford to Southall, which together with the service from the West Midlands to Southall still operates twice a day in each direction. (RS)

I know I said earlier that it was unusual for municipal operators to purchase buses from independents, but here's another one... Eastbourne Buses Duple Dominant bus-bodied B10M 19 (D499 NYS) was new in 1986 to Hutchison of Overtown, an operator who had a penchant for Dominant bus-bodied vehicles. It is seen passing Eastbourne railway station in 1993. (AS)

The impressive Plaxton Paramount 4000 was available as a full double-decker, or when fitted to mid-engined chassis such as the B10MT became what was in effect a super-high single-deck coach with a small rear lounge, although the presence of the lounge meant that they had to be licensed as double-deck coaches. 6690 DD was new to Davies Bros of Pencader as D388 FBX, and is seen parked on Victoria Embankment, being the regular performer on their London service. (PG)

At the other end of the Paramount scale is a B9M I remember from my time in Bristol. First Streamline's Paramount 3200-bodied 8752 (E752 YDY) was new to Airport Parking, Gatwick in 1988, and was purchased by First as a dual-role vehicle, its short length and manual gearbox making it ideal for loaning to the driver-training school where my dad was a member of the instruction team. It is undertaking such duties when seen parked on Manvers Street across from Bath bus station. (RS)

Just as SYPTE had the Ailsa demonstrator on loan, its successor South Yorkshire Transport had the Ailsa's successor on loan. Alexander-bodied Citybus E825 OMS is seen on Far Lane, East Dene while on loan to Rotherham depot. After its demonstration days were over, it joined Nottingham City Transport as number 330. (RS)

I always found it rather odd that from producing such gracefully curvaceous bodies as the 'Y' and 'M' types, Alexander should choose to make the 'P' type such an angular and boxy affair. Despite its looks, the 'P' type was a rugged and soundly constructed beast, and when fitted with semi-coach seats and with the B10M under it, would be up to any task. Proof is here, with Burnely & Pendle's 65 (E65 JFV) having made the trip from 'oop north to dahn sarf', arriving at Wembley in 1990. (AS)

London-based Frames-Rickards was formed in 1967 when Charles Rickards (Tours) Ltd became a subsidiary of Frames Tours Ltd, both being old established coach operators. In 1894 Charles Rickards was appointed as Posting Master to Queen Victoria and in 1936 was awarded the Royal Warrant, and this was retained when the new company was formed. For many years they operated the Heathrow–Woking Railair link, and Plaxton Paramount 3200-bodied B10M E169 OMD is seen departing Heathrow in 1990. (AS)

E364 NEG was new to Premier Travel of Cambridge in 1988, fitted with a Plaxton Paramount 3200 body. Following an accident in which the coach was rolled on the M11, the body was scrapped, and the chassis acquired by Tillingbourne, who had a new Northern Counties bus body fitted. It is seen outside The Friary shopping centre in Guildford. (AS)

In 1988, upon privatisation from the NBC, my then employer Western National went on a buying spree, purchasing an eclectic mix of new vehicles, including three coach-seated Alexander-bodied Citybuses, primarily for use on the Plymouth to Exeter/Torquay services. As Western National was part of the Badgerline Group, all three eventually transferred to Bristol, and E215 BTA is seen exiting St James Barton roundabout en route to Marlborough Street bus station. (AS)

When Grey-Green won the tender to operate LRT route 24, it brought the first non-red buses to operate regular services into the centre of London for a long time. Grey-Green wanted to ensure that this new operation would be a media success, so no tatty second-hand buses would do. They spent over £2.5 million on thirty new Alexander-bodied Citybuses in a striking new livery of grey, green (what else!) and orange. 142 (F142 PHM) is seen entering Parliament Square from Whitehall in 1989. (AS)

Isle Coaches of Owston Ferry are one of the few South Yorkshire independent bus operators still in existence and operate a small network of services based around Doncaster. In excellent condition for its nigh on twenty-year age, Alexander-bodied Citybus F137 PHM, formerly Grey-Green number 137, passes Keadby Bridge on its afternoon run from John Leggott College, Scunthorpe in 2007. (RS)

In the lead-up to deregulation, Alder Valley was split into two. The northern division was renamed The Berks Bucks Bus Co., trading as The Bee Line, adopting a yellow and grey livery adorned with bees. In 1987, it was sold to Q Drive, a company set up by Len Wright, and in 1989 ten Jonckheere Jubilee-bodied B10Ms arrived for use on the Londonlink services. 783 (F773 OJH) is seen arriving at VCS shortly after delivery. (AS)

The only vehicles delivered to post-deregulation Southdown prior to takeover by Stagecoach were twelve Northern Counties-bodied Citybuses in 1989. They were fitted with coach seats for use on the 700 Brighton to Southsea service, however 306 (F306 MYJ), seen here, is picking up in South Street, Worthing en route to Littlehampton. (AS)

Founded in 1907, Finglands of Rusholme at one time operated Finglands Airways, using two Avro Ansons. Passengers were collected by coach from their homes in Manchester and taken to the airfield and flown to Newquay. There, another Finglands coach would take them to their hotel and then undertake day trips. On deregulation, they were one of the first operators to run dedicated low-fare buses for students along the busy Wilmslow Road. Seen taking Manchester United supporters to Wembley is Alexander-bodied Citybus 710 (F242 MBA), new to Finglands in 1989. (AS)

Whippet of Fenstanton was founded by bicycle salesman Henry Lee in 1919, his first coach being a converted American ambulance. The company went on to become one of the largest independents in Cambridgeshire, operating an extensive network of stage services using a fleet of new and second-hand double-deckers. Seen leaving Cambridge bus station is Northern Counties-bodied Citybus G823 UMU, one of a pair bought new in 1989. (AS)

A coach I remember very well from my National Express days was Speedlink's Plaxton Paramount 3500-bodied B10M VP1 (G801 BPG), known as 'Gatwick Girl'. New in 1989, it only seated thirty-five and was used solely for transferring Virgin Atlantic aircrew between airports. It is seen being prepared for service at London & Country's Crawley garage in 1993. (AS)

A varied line of double-deckers at Imperial Coaches' Colnbrook yard, with both East Lancs-bodied Citybuses having been given front-end makeovers. A5 VXH was formerly London & Country G616 BPH while A2 VXH was ex-North Western G641 CHF. Also present are an ex-Lothian Volvo Olympian and an ex-Metroline Dennis Trident. (PG)

The 1990s – A Decade of Change

After the success of the 1980s, culminating in the takeover of Leyland Bus in 1988, the start of the 1990s saw a period of retrenchment – completely understandable for a company that now had two comparable product ranges and multiple manufacturing facilities. Whereas the Volvo catalogue consisted of basically one chassis, Leyland's included four single-deckers and two double-deckers, one being the very popular Olympian. By the mid-1990s, the entire Leyland range had been discontinued, however the Olympian name was retained and given to an almost completely new Volvo-designed double-decker, manufactured in a brand-new assembly hall in Irvine built at a cost of £6.5 million. The Volvo Olympian was based on its Leyland predecessor, but was so vastly modified that only the chassis layout remained, with even the grade of steel for the chassis members being changed. Volvo's electrical system, steering, braking system and standard dashboard layout were all now used. Early Volvo Olympians were offered with either the Cummins L10 or Volvo TD102KF engine, but from 1996 only the 9.6-litre Volvo D10A was offered. So popular had the B10M become that, prior to its closure, the former Leyland factory in Workington, Cumbria was used to manufacture right-hand drive B10Ms due to the main assembly plant at Boras in Sweden running at maximum capacity and being unable to satisfy orders generated from former Leyland customers. Talking of the B10M, 1990 saw the first mainstream deliveries of the Expressliner, a joint venture between Volvo, Plaxton and National Express. Based on the B10M MkIII chassis and fitted with a Plaxton Paramount 3500 body, the Expressliner was kitted out to National Express' specification, with the National Express 'N sign' on all moquette and interior furnishings, and embossed into a detachable moulded panel that completely covered the rear of the coach. Available as 'Rapide' containing forty-six seats, servery, and toilet; and standard, with forty-nine seats and toilet, Expressliners were available via direct purchase or through a leasing arrangement via Kirkby's, Plaxton's dealer network. At the end of the lease, the coaches were returned to Kirkby's for refurbishment, removing all traces of National Express, including removal of the moulded rear-end cover to reveal the rear window. To run alongside the B10M, in 1994 Volvo introduced the B12T to the UK. The B12T was a tri-axle rear-engined chassis, the majority of which were bodied as double-deck coaches – many finding use on National Express operations.

By the start of the 1990s, operators were starting to shed the degree of caution shown following deregulation, and new single-deck bus orders started to increase, particularly from one operator. Back in the 1980s, Volvo had been approached by one of the proprietors of a small, newly formed Scottish company who had purchased a new B58 that suffered engine failure when just out of warranty. As a goodwill gesture, Sandy Glennie, then MD of Volvo Bus, offered them a replacement engine and made probably the best decision of his career, as that small Scottish operator was Stagecoach, a company that went on to become one of the largest transport groups in the world. Stagecoach made the B10M their standard single-decker, and when specified for bus work their B10Ms were built to a unique specification, with the THD101 engine rated at 212bhp, the majority receiving

Alexander 'PS' bodies. For inter-urban coach work, Plaxton or Jonckheere were the preferred coachbuilders, both supplying several B10MA 'bendicoaches'.

The 1980s saw the introduction of minibuses on high frequency routes going 'off the beaten track' to serve locations such as housing estates that were inaccessible to full-sized vehicles. The popularity of such services saw passenger numbers rising, meaning larger vehicles still able to traverse the new routes were required. Enter the midibus, Volvo's offering being the step-entrance B6, introduced in 1991 as competition to the popular Dennis Dart, Stagecoach being the first to order the B6 in large numbers. It was powered by a 5.5-litre engine and available in 8.5-, 9.0-, and 9.9-metre lengths. In 1995, the B6LE with a 350-mm low-entry floor was added, and two years later the entire step-entrance range was discontinued. The B6LE was itself replaced in 1999 by the B6BLE, with a lower chassis frame, increased low-floor area, independent front suspension giving a wider gangway between the front wheel arches, and front-end 'kneeling', allowing an entrance height of just 25 cm.

A year after the B6 was introduced, it became evident why the popular Leyland Lynx had been discontinued when, at the 1992 Geneva Motor Show, Volvo launched the B10B, a full-length rear-engined step-entrance single-decker chassis, which was initially powered by the DH10A engine. However, a major factor influencing bus design to how we know it today was the growing requirement for accessible buses, ideally with wheelchair entry directly from the kerb and flat floors throughout. In 1993 Volvo introduced the B10L, a rear-engined low-floor single-decker, with an articulated version (B10LA) also available. The B10L was only available with Alexander (Belfast) Ultra and Wright bodies, with the Ultra marketed by Volvo itself, based on a design produced by Säffle, a subsidiary of Volvo. The Wright body was more popular, and for UK use the only B10LAs were bodied by Wright's exclusively for FirstGroup. In 1997 a low-floor version of the B10B, the B10BLE, was introduced to the UK, quickly becoming more popular than the B10L, not only due to its price but also due to sharing many components with the B10B, examples of which were already owned by many of its potential customers. Both the B10L and B10BLE were available with CNG (compressed natural gas) power as well as conventional diesel. The final model to reach the UK in 1997 was the B7R, a fully air-suspended rear-engined coach chassis, ideal as both an inter-urban express coach or a lighter weight luxury coach. Powered by the 6.7-litre D7B230 intercooled engine and fitted with a ZF six-speed manual gearbox as standard, although automatic transmission was offered as an option, the B7R was intended to complement the B10M rather than compete against it.

In 1989, attempting to bring uniformity to the coaches used on its network, National Express collaborated with Volvo and Plaxton to produce the Expressliner. Essentially a Plaxton Paramount 3500-bodied B10M, but built to National Express's own specification, it was easily recognisable from the standard Paramount by having a windowless rear end incorporating the National Express logo. One of the first, and a coach I did many miles in, was G995 XHW, delivered to Wessex of Bristol in 1990 and seen departing VCS for home in 1991. (AS)

Following deregulation, Shearings threw themselves heavily into local bus operation, running services across northern England, the Midlands and the South East. Delivered new in 1991, Alexander 'N' type-bodied B10M H78 DVM picks up in Midland Street, Barnsley while running in competition against Yorkshire Traction on service 111 to Athersley North. (RS)

In 1986, London & Country won several LRT contracts, and initially operated them with a fleet of second-hand Leyland Atlanteans acquired from Scotland, Manchester, and Tyneside. The fine citizens of inner Surrey (L&C's main operating area) didn't want cast-off buses transporting their wives, children and servants, so the company had to update its fleet if it was to renew its existing contracts, let alone win new ones. To operate the 176 from Oxford Circus to Penge, a batch of East Lancs-bodied Citybuses was ordered, including 674 (H674 GPF), new in 1990. (AS)

It was almost unheard of for a coach built at the start of this book's time frame to be air conditioned, but during the 1990s, more operators specified it as an option and nowadays it's taken as a standard fitment. Before technological advancements saw the air-con units become compact enough to be hidden within the bodywork, it was commonplace to fit it onto the roof, as can be seen on Van Hool Alizee-bodied B10M J19 UST of Just Travel of Tadcaster. The coach was new to Tappin's of Didcot in 1993 as K301 GDT. (RS)

Sheffield Omnibus was formed by a group of former Preston Bus employees to compete against South Yorkshire Transport. Originally running elderly Leyland Atlanteans on cross-city services in Sheffield, the company adopted Preston's livery, which was similar to the pre-1974 Sheffield Transport livery. SYT's arch competitor Yorkshire Traction subsequently acquired Sheffield Omnibus, with the first bus bought new being Alexander 'PS' type B10M 235 (K235 MAP), seen preparing to leave the depot at Ecclesfield. (RS)

In 1992, London General received fourteen B10Bs fitted with Northern Counties Paladin bodies to operate route 88 from Oxford Circus to Clapham Common, branded as 'The Clapham Omnibus'. Allocated to Stockwell depot, they were unpopular with passengers due to being fitted with rather uncomfortable bucket seats, and four years after delivery were all sold to the Oxford Bus Company. VN8 (K8 KLL) is seen rounding Parliament Square in Westminster. (AS)

I'm not sure whether the driver on Burnley & Pendle's East Lancs-bodied B10M 426 (K26 WBV) is waving nicely at the photographer or is just a little bit camera shy! Seen on Yorkshire Street in Burnley, it was one of four such vehicles delivered in 1993, all built to the uncommon 10-metre length with seating for forty-five. (RS)

When Plaxton replaced the Paramount range with the Premiere in 1992, National Express were quick to work with Plaxton to produce the Expressliner 2, based on the high-line Premiere 350 and again using the B10M. Seen at VCS is K3 CEN, from the Central Coachways fleet, Central being the coaching arm of West Midlands PTE who for many years operated a joint service with London Coaches between Birmingham and London in competition with National Express. (AS)

For decades, the Shropshire-based Whittle Group was almost 100 per cent Bedford, with hundreds entering the group's fleets over the years. With the closure of Bedford, the Dennis Javelin became the favoured chassis but in 1993, three Plaxton Premiere 350-bodied B10Ms including K36 OUY were delivered. The early build Premieres suffered teething problems, not least with the cantilever-style boot door which would come away from the body when driven at speed! (AS)

The first Plaxton Premieres built were delivered to Wallace Arnold, who became so concerned with the build quality that they explored other options for their deliveries from 1993 onwards. Seen parked in the Burlington Hotel in Eastbourne is Jonckheere Deauville-bodied B10M L944 NWW, one of forty-seven similar vehicles delivered over a two-year period. (AS)

Seen carrying a special livery for the GNER Railink service between Bradford and Wakefield is Yorkshire Rider's Jonckheere Deauville-bodied B10M 1422 (YR 3939). New in 1993 as L22 YRL, it later passed to Kee Travel of Normanton. Today, there are direct train services between Bradford and Wakefield operated by Grand Central, but when things go awry and coaches are required to replace trains, GC's preferred operator is... Kee Travel. (RS)

Volvo's response to the midibus boom of the mid-1990s was the B6, powered by a 5.5-litre engine and built at Volvo's brand-new bus chassis plant in Irvine, Scotland. On a miserable wet day in Pontypridd, Bebb's Marshall-bodied L82 CNY, one of six delivered in 1994, is seen waiting to depart to Beddau. After a short life with Bebbs, it returned to Volvo and was loaned for a while to First Glasgow before being sold to Lincolnshire Road Car. (RS)

The look of the Northern Counties Paladin body with its gently sloped side windows was spoiled slightly when a destination box was incorporated into the first side window, but completely ruined when the destination box was later panelled over. New to Capital Citybus, B6 L888 AMY later passed to First Leicester, where it can be seen wearing the short-lived green, yellow and white livery a small number of vehicles received in 2000. (RS)

Englands most westerly operator is Mounts Bay Coaches of Marazion in Cornwall, named after the beautiful Cornish landmark of St Michael's Mount, which sits magnificently behind the company's depot. Tidy Van Hool Alizee-bodied B9M XIL 4290 'Cap'n Poldark' was new to Armchair as L116 OWF and is seen about to arrive home in 2019. (PG)

Displaying its B9M badging is Berkhof Excellence-bodied L300 SUP, new to Supreme of Hadleigh in 1994. Photographed in Doncaster coach park, it was suffering a slight identity crisis, as despite carrying the livery and fleet name of Milligan of Mauchline it was being operated by White Star of Houghton-le-Spring. (RS)

The 1990s saw the start of the corporate livery within the larger groups, the rationale being that vehicles transferred inter-fleet could become operational straight away rather than waiting for repaint. Stagecoach adopted the Alexander 'PS' bodied B10M as their standard single-decker and seen here in Eastbourne is a good example of an inter-fleet transfer. 616 (L616 TDY) was new to Stagecoach South Coast, but also operated in the Devon and Merseyside fleets. (AS)

National Express routes, primarily those to Devon and Cornwall, were (and still are) double-deck operated due to high levels of passenger loadings. As these only accounted for a small percentage of the network, there wasn't a double-deck Expressliner, leaving operators free to choose the type of vehicles operated. By the time Van Hool Astrobel-bodied B12B M864 TYC had been delivered to Trathen's, the company had risen from the ashes and was one of National Express's largest contract operators. (RS)

One football transfer that didn't make the newspapers was Grayscroft of Mablethorpe's Caetano Algarve-bodied B10M RJI 1653, which was new in 1994 to Nottingham Forest FC as their team coach. Originally registered M488 HBC, it is seen in Doncaster on rail replacement work. (RS)

While the B6 was built primarily as a midibus: fifteen were bodied as coaches, five by Jonckheere and ten by Caetano. Godson's of Crossgates took delivery of Caetano Algarve-bodied M955 HRY in 1994, its smaller wheels making the body look slightly top-heavy. (RS)

With not a jot of lettering to identify its operator is Trent's Alexander Q type-bodied B10M M52 PRA. En route to Nottingham on the Trans Peak service from Manchester, it has just passed under Buxton's impressive railway viaduct. (MH)

The one place where corporate identity did not feature was in London, with red being the order of the day for buses working into the capital. Stagecoach acquired Selkent in 1994, and its priority was to replace the ageing Leyland Titans on service 53 (Plumstead Station to Trafalgar Square). Stagecoach chose Cummins-powered, Northern Counties-bodied Volvo Olympians, and 308 (M308 DGP) is seen at Blackheath when new. (AS)

The 1990s saw the start of the shift towards accessible low-floor buses, and in 1994 Volvo introduced the rear-engined B10L. It was only available under the Wright Liberator and Alexander (Belfast) Ultra, the latter marketed by Volvo and based on a design by Volvo subsidiary Säffle. L456 JCK, the first UK B10L, was actually bodied by Säffle and was placed on extended loan from Volvo to Mainline. It is seen here in Sheffield. (RS)

The B10L was able to be powered by diesel or compressed natural gas (CNG), with only Travel West Midlands and First Northampton taking the CNG option. New in 1997, Northampton's 506 (P506 MVV) advertises its power credentials as well as those of the various companies involved in the Gas Bus project. (RS)

In the early 1990s, Shearings sold off their bus fleet to concentrate on their coaching operations, resulting in the formation of Timeline Travel. Timeline developed quite a network across the Greater Manchester and Cheshire area before selling to First Manchester in 1998. 303 (N303 WNF) was one of six Alexander Ultra-bodied B10Ls to join the fleet. (RS)

The rear-engined B10B was intended as the replacement for the Leyland Lynx, which was Travel West Midlands' standard single-decker. They ordered just over fifty B10Bs, all fitted with Wright Endurance bodywork including 1332 (N332 WHO), seen in Wolverhampton. (RS)

A nice line-up of First Kernow Olympians seen parked at the Eden Project in St Austell. 34261 (N542 LHG) and 31826 (P926 RYO) have the original style of Northern Counties Palatine bodies, while 34051 (P251 UCW) has the Palatine II. 34194 (481 FPO, ex N113 UHP), the odd man out, has an Alexander Royale body. All were cascaded to Cornwall from London Buses subsidiaries. (PG)

Formed in 1988 when the former NBC subsidiary West Yorkshire Road Car Co. was split into smaller units by its new owner the AJS Group, Harrogate & District has seen some changes. Sold in 1991 to Blazefield Travel, then again in 2006 to Transdev, where it was rebranded 'Transdev in Harrogate', its last change was in 2016 when it became The Harrogate Bus Company. Seen during Blazefield ownership is Wright Crusader-bodied B6LE 643 (P643 UUG), new in 1997. (RS)

Well-respected Lincolnshire operator Delaine of Bourne operate a network of services from Bourne to Spalding, Stamford and Peterborough and are one of the few independent operators still purchasing brand-new service buses. However, a second-hand purchase from an unlikely source was Wright Endurance-bodied P87 SAF, new to Cornish operator Hopley's of Mount Hawke. (MH)

And talking of Hopley's, here's one of the current fleet. Seen climbing St Clement's Hill in Truro and looking immaculate for its near twenty-five years is this former Clarkes of London Jonckheere Deauville-bodied B10M. Formerly N539 SJF, it is now registered YAF 65, a good old Cornish number plate for a good old Cornish company. (PG)

Before the arrival of children put an end to any form of enjoyment, the current Mrs Berry and I had numerous holidays based in the small Lakes village of Glenridding, so it was nice to find this picture of Stagecoach Alexander PS-bodied B10M 20965 (R965 XVM) about to arrive there. The bus will travel about a mile beyond Glenridding to the small settlement of Patterdale, but in the more tourist-rich months, the service is extended over the Kirkstone Pass to Windermere. (MH)

I know it's from the same batch as above, but I had to include R928 XVM to show that 'where there's a will, there's a way'. After several weeks of 'fag packet' development work by photo contributor MH and his team, this B10M 'cabriolet' emerged from the workshop in 2013. It was created at the behest of Quantock Motor Services to operate their service from Minehead to Lynmouth. (MH)

One of East Anglia's largest independent operators was Hedingham & District, based in the Essex village of Sible Hedingham. Steady expansion over the years saw Hedingham take over some of the area's well-know independents such as Osborne of Tollesbury and Partridge of Hadleigh, before selling to the Go-Ahead Group in 2012. Seen in Colchester shortly after the takeover is ex-Brighton & Hove Wright Renown-bodied B10BLE L412 (R233 HCD). (PG)

Volvo introduced the lightweight rear-engined B7R in 1998 and had R342 EDB fitted with a Plaxton Prima body to use as a Volvo/Plaxton demonstrator. The Prima was externally identical to the Premiere 320 but with a lower specification interior. Its time spent on demonstration with Shearings obviously didn't work as the company didn't order any Primas or B7s. (RS)

Shearings did, however, continue to buy the B10M, and like Wallace Arnold (their rivals at the time), had them bodied by Van Hool and Jonckheere. As can be seen in this shot of Jonckheere Mistral-bodied 937 (R937 YNF) parked outside the King's Head Hotel in Cirencester, Shearings had changed their livery to mainly blue, probably how most of the passengers were feeling looking at the state of the weather... (RS)

Another Jonckheere Mistral-bodied B10M, but this time the old 9-metre-long 'B9M' variant is Glenn Ryder Coaches of Mansfield's R100 GRC. It was new to Kerry Tours of Killarney in 1998-registered 98-KY-2442. (RS)

When the batch of twenty-eight Northern Counties-bodied Olympians delivered to Arriva Midlands in 1998 were disposed of, they really did get sold to operators across the length and breadth of England and Wales. The one that went the furthest west was R634 MNU, joining the fleet of F.T. Williams of Camborne, a company well known when I was 'behind the wheel' in Cornwall for having a lovely pair of Bristols – Plaxton-bodied REs. Appearing to have suffered damage to its upper offside, it is seen in the village of Portreath. (PG)

Dusk falls as C&G Coaches of Chatteris' East Lancs Pyoneer-bodied Olympian S461 ATV returns to the yard from its afternoon school run. New to Nottingham City Transport (who had some of the first Volvo Olympians built) as fleet number 461 in 1999, it arrived in Cambridgeshire via Scotland, having operated with Irvine of Law and Stuarts of Carluke. (PG)

Another East Lancs Pyoneer-bodied Olympian is S858 DGX, new to Metrobus for operating LRT tendered route 118. With a requirement for low-floor buses on LRT routes on the horizon, Metrobus wisely leased their Olympians. Seen here being operated by my friends the Keeber family in the fleet of G. H. Watts of Leicester, and now registered S33 GHW, it has probably never looked as good as this before. (PG)

Bendibuses have never been popular in the UK, and apart from a handful running around South Yorkshire in the 1970s and 1980s, it wasn't until the late 1990s that any were delivered in significant numbers, when forty Wright Fusion-bodied B10LAs buses were delivered to FirstGroup. They were split between the Glasgow, Yorkshire, and Manchester fleets, with Manchester's 2001 (S111 FML) being the first to be delivered. It is seen on layover in a very wet Bury bus station. (RS)

Stagecoach ordered 'bendicoaches' for use on their services, and so went for the higher-floor B10MA fitted with Jonckheere or Plaxton bodies, with some operating the overnight sleeper service between Glasgow and London. Slightly less glamorous but successful enough to justify articulated coaches was Stagecoach Express service 909. Jonckheere Modulo-bodied T96 JHN is loading in Grimsby bus station for the journey to Sheffield. (RS)

The good people of Saint-Quentin in northern France are lucky enough to be twinned with Rotherham and in 2001 were even luckier to be visited by Mainline Wright Renown-bodied B10BLE 822 (T822 MAK). It is seen alongside 8555 VT 02, a Renault Agora, fleet no. 41 in the fleet of local operator TUSQ. (RS)

Two former stablemates are reunited in this shot taken in the 'independent' parking area in the late lamented Bretonside bus station in Plymouth. Both are ex-Wallace Arnold Plaxton Premiere 350-bodied B10Ms, T544 EUB on the left owned by Turner's Tours of Chulmleigh in Devon, while Cornish operator Roselyn of Par's 239 AJB (originally fitted to a Park Royal-bodied AEC Regent V new to the UK Atomic Energy Research Establishment) was new as T523 EUB. (PG)

With a full-width body but smaller wheels, the B6 always looked a little 'top-heavy'. Sheffield Community Transport's Wright Crusader 2-bodied B6BLE T506 TOL is named *Benjamin Huntsman*, a Sheffield inventor whose experiments led to him creating cast steel. New to Airlinks, it is seen pulling out of Hillsborough interchange. (RS)

As earlier photographs have shown, the big groups such as First, Arriva and Stagecoach insisted on corporate livery unless operational circumstances dictated otherwise, so it is surprising that Alexander-bodied B7TL 32027 (OIG 1794) in the First Kernow fleet has not one jot of FirstGroup identification on it. New to London General in 2000 as AVL24 (V124 LGC), it is seen leaving Penzance bus station for Land's End in 2018. (PG)

Into the New Millennium

The new millennium saw a move towards a greener, cleaner environment. Engines were designed to be less pollutive, with European Union regulations set for manufacturers to meet more stringent emissions targets. Congestion charges and low-emission zones became commonplace across Europe, and Volvo were determined to be one of the first manufacturers to be compliant. Diesel engines became smaller in size, but leaner and more economical, and the race to find an alternative fuel to diesel came to the fore. The Volvo B10BLE had been a success, however when it came to meeting the latest Euro III regulations, Volvo chose to return to the B10M concept and, in an attempt to produce a chassis that could be bodied as a single-deck or double-deck bus, introduced the fully low-floor rear-engined B7L. Intended to replace the B10L, B10BLE and Olympian, its 7.3-litre engine was mounted vertically on the left-hand side of the chassis overhang with the radiator mounted above it to allow the floor to be lower behind the rear axle. Unfortunately, this unusual layout didn't endear it to many operators; the engine enclosed in a kind of 'shower cubicle' that encroached into the saloon was not only noisy, but also reduced seating capacity. On the double-deck version, the engine layout led to a particularly long rear overhang, and despite its best intentions both versions of the B7L only sold to a handful of operators. An unusual application on the B7LA (the articulated version of the B7L) were the Wright StreetCar-bodied vehicles built for FirstGroup for the FTR project. The leading axle was moved to the extreme front of the vehicle and the driver (or pilot) sat in a cabin above the axle, separated from the rest of the vehicle. With fully enclosed wheels and wrap-around seating at the rear, they were designed to emulate continental streetcars. Their main areas of operation were Yorkshire and South Wales but they failed to impress, and withdrawals started when they were less than six years old.

The B7L was replaced by the B7RLE single-deck, and the B7TL double-deck, fitted with a transverse engine to reduce the overall length, both of which were much more popular than their predecessor, and the last B7TLs were delivered in 2007, having been replaced in 2005 by the B9TL. This shared the same chassis design as the B7TL, the main difference being a Renault-designed 9.3-litre engine. Originally offered only as a tri-axle double-decker, the two-axle variant was added in 2006 to replace the B7TL. The B9TL was originally fitted with the D9A Euro III engine rated at either 300bhp or 340bhp, but subsequently the D9B Euro IV/V/EEV engine that used selective catalytic reduction technology was added. Two versions were available: the D9B260 rated at 260bhp for two-axle version, and the higher-powered D9B310, rated at 310bhp, for the tri-axle. Both were coupled to a ZF five/six-speed gearbox with the Voith four-speed gearbox as an option.

For coachwork, Volvo introduced the B12M and B12B. The B12M was a direct replacement for the B10M, and retained the same basic layout, complete with the side-mounted radiator, but was fitted with the more powerful 12-litre DH12 engine. The B12B was a new model altogether, with its DH12 engine fitted at the rear, and was available as a two- or three- (B12BT) axle luxury coach. The chassis was supplied in modular form with all major components behind the rear and ahead of the front axle, allowing bodybuilders to arrange the underfloor luggage area to suit their or their customers' requirements. Both B12M and B12B were available with manual or fully automatic gearboxes and remained in production throughout the first decade of the new century.

I speak from experience when I say that route branding is great when you have enough vehicles to cover service, but a traffic office nightmare when the only spare bus is branded for a route it's not running on. Originally branded as BOB (Bright Orange Buses) so the students knew which colour bus to catch (yep, I'm serious...) the service between Bath University and the city centre now runs as UNIBUS, as seen on First West of England's Wright Fusion-bodied B7LA 10037 (W122 CWR). (PG)

Talking of route branding, in 2003 National Express merged its AirLink, FlightLink, Speedlink and Jetlink operations together under the National Express 'Airport' banner, the four constituents losing their individual liveries. Showing the new branding is Plaxton Panther-bodied B10M W208 EAG, passing Tower Gateway DLR station en route to Stansted in 2005. (PG)

The Nottinghamshire village of Cropwell Bishop is home to one of only six dairies in the world licensed to make Stilton cheese, and at the time of writing is also home to something else rather tasty – the immaculate fleet of Sharpe's of Nottingham. With the sun glinting off its polished wheeltrims, Alexander ALX400-bodied B7TL SIL 706 is seen departing the Yorkshire Wildlife Park. New in 2000 as Dublin Bus AV40 and registered 00-D-40040, it arrived with Sharpe's in 2015. (RS)

A few years ago, the Berrys took a very wet holiday in Whitby, and what do you do when it's horsing down with rain? You take an open-top bus tour! We boarded Coastal & Country's ageing Leyland Olympian, which threw all its drive belts on the long climb up to Whitby Abbey. To the rescue came their ex-London General Plaxton President-bodied B7TL Y738 TGH. The next day I (foolishly) climbed the 199 steps up to the abbey, to find the Olympian still abandoned at the side of the road. (PG)

In 2001, Go Whippet of Fenstanton received four East Lancs-bodied Volvos. One, a B7TL double-decker, the other three being B6BLEs, and two of the three including FE51 RBU are seen in St Ives bus station in 2012. Two years later, and after ninety-five years of continuous family ownership, Go Whippet would be sold to Tower Transit. (PG)

Another long-serving family business was France's Motors of Market Weighton, formed in 1927 using Ideal Motor Services for the coaches, and R&J France for the haulage fleet. The two were amalgamated in 1971, and operations continued until the France brothers retired in 2011, selling the business to York Pullman. In 2018, York Pullman painted Wright Renown-bodied B10M Y161 HRN into Ideal's colours, and it is seen in Pocklington heading for Woldgate. (RS)

The majority of bus services in rural areas don't tend to be operated by fleets operating newly purchased state-of-the-art buses, but one company bucking that trend is DRM of Bromyard. Back in 2001, DRM purchased DM51 BUS, an East Lancs Spryte-bodied Volvo B6BLE, and it is seen in Hereford bus station when new. (RS)

TM Travel was founded in Chesterfield in 1995 as a family-owned operation running one coach. A move into local bus services saw the fleet increase in size to over 100 vehicles in just over ten years, making it the largest independent operator in Derbyshire. In 2010 it was taken over by the Wellglade Group, owner of notable former East Midlands independents such as Barton and Kinchbus. Transbus Profile-bodied B7R YN03 WXS is seen passing through the centre of Derby. (RS)

Roselyn Coaches of Par has always been dear to me; it was here I first became involved in the industry many moons ago, helping clean coaches in the school holidays. The family connection with Roselyn remains, as my brother is the man responsible for carrying out all the signwriting on the fleet. With a registration to honour William Bryan Ede, the father of Jonathan, the current owner, Van Hool Alizee-bodied B12M WB03 EDE is seen travelling through Bath. (RS)

With similar East Lancs bodywork on different makes of chassis, Stagecoach 16909 and 18283 meet at the exit to Lincoln bus station. 16909 on the right is a B7TL acquired new by Lincolnshire Road Car, while 18283 approaching from the left is a Dennis Trident that was new to Bullock of Cheadle and transferred from Stagecoach Manchester. (RS)

A wonderfully artistic photograph of L777 KMP, a Wright-bodied B7RLE of KMP, Llanberis. I remember KMP from when they operated into London Victoria on behalf of Bus Eireann, but they also ran an extensive network of bus services across North Wales before being purchased, partly by Arriva Cymru, with the majority passing to Llanberis operator Padarn in 2009. (MH)

A couple of years ago, in a fit of nostalgia, FirstGroup allowed operating companies to repaint some vehicles in 'heritage' liveries. Seen in Bath is First West of England's offering, Wright-bodied B7RLE 66726 (WX54 XDK) in Badgerline livery, which might seem modern to some, but it's over thirty years ago that the livery first appeared. (PG)

My old employer First Potteries chose several different heritage liveries including this pre-NBC version on Wright Gemini-bodied B7TL 32634 (KP54 LAO). Seen in Hanley, it was new to sister Midland's company First Northampton in 2005, and is dedicated to the memory of Ernest Albert Egerton, a First World War VC recipient who was born in the Potteries town of Longton. (PG)

The days of the open-top bus being a time-expired double-decker with its roof lopped off are long gone, as shown by RATP Bath Bus Company's 381 (EU04 CPV). New to the company in 2004, the Ayats Bravo City-bodied B7L is waiting time outside The Huntsman on North Parade in Bath, which if I remember rightly serves a cracking pint of London Pride. (PG)

The three routes Go South Coast's New Forest tour operates over are all colour coded, with vehicles painted to match the route. The red route runs a circular tour from Lyndhurst via the quaintly named Sandy Balls Holiday Centre. I stayed there for the 1991 Coach Driver of the Year competition and the name still makes me snigger. East Lancs-bodied B7TL 1824 (HF54 KXW) departs Ringwood on the last day of operation in 2019. (PG)

Unveiled in August 1882, the imposing statue of Catholic emancipator Daniel O'Connell looks down on O'Connell Street in Dublin. The monument was designed and sculpted by John Henry Foley and finished by his assistant, Thomas Brock. Dublin Bus B7TL AV425 (05-D-10425), however, was designed by Volvo, and finished by Alexander with an ALX 400 body. (PG)

As a teenager, I spent many a happy hour sitting in Yelloway's Weir Street coach station, surrounded by those elegant orange and yellow AEC Reliances and Leyland Leopards. Sadly, both Weir Street and the original Yelloway are nothing but fond memories. However Chadderton-based Courtesy Coaches have revived the Yelloway name. With the famous logo emblazoned on its side is Plaxton Paragon-bodied B12B M70 YEL, new to the company in 2005 as YN54 WWA. (RS)

During my time at Wessex of Bristol, I was involved in one of the biggest changes in terms of frequency and vehicle used when the service from Bristol bus station to Bristol airport went from running once an hour using an Iveco minibus, to every ten minutes using full-size coaches. Seen passing the former head office of the Bristol Tramways & Carriage Co. after Wessex had morphed into First Coaches is Plaxton Profile-bodied B7R 20307 (WX05 OZF). (RS)

There can't be many independent operators whose fleet comprises almost entirely Volvo single-deck buses, but Reliance of Sutton-on-the-Forest is one. Reliance have been providing bus services across North Yorkshire for over ninety years and seen standing in Thirsk's beautiful marketplace is Wright Eclipse Urban-bodied B7RLE BV55 UAZ, originally used by Volvo as a demonstrator. (RS)

It's funny how the addition of an extra axle can make a bus look bigger than it actually is, a good example being this photo of Seaford & District's 12-metre-long Alexander Enviro 500-bodied B9TL LW55 CDZ. New to Dublin Bus as V2 (05-D-70002), it is seen on private hire duty in Battle. (PG)

When I worked for Sanders of Holt, we trundled round East Anglia in Plaxton- or Duple-bodied Bedfords, not stonking great things like *Goliath*, and with seats for 102 passengers, he carries nearly twice as many as those Bedfords. Y14 BUS is an East Lancs Millenium Nordic-bodied B9TL, new as OU05 KLA, along with five similar vehicles to Weavaway of Newbury. (PG)

Here's the proof that FirstGroup painted buses on the Bath University service orange so the students could recognise them. Despite the destination confirming its colour, and route branding on the sides, some students would STILL ask which bus was theirs. Unlike the advertising slogan for the mobile network of the same colour, for some of them, the future certainly wasn't bright. Wright Eclipse Fusion-bodied B7LA 10182 (WX55 HWH) later passed to First Northampton for use at Luton Airport. (RS)

I obviously enjoyed my time working for Sanders of Holt as I had to drive past three other companies just to get there. Only one is still with us, the small but perfectly formed Sunbeam of Hevingham. I was including this photograph of 9700 N27 SUN in Portsmouth en route to the Isle of Wight anyway, but by pure coincidence it started life as the other of the two 2005 demonstrators, this one registered VL05 VBL. (PG)

In 1997 Volvo purchased the Finnish bodybuilder Carros Oy, and in 2001 introduced the 9700 range. The first two to enter the UK were Volvo's 2005 demonstration coaches, and the appropriately registered VL05 VOL is seen here in Blackpool while being used by Baker's of Biddulph. (PG)

Another Jonckheere Mistral, but this time on a B12M, is from my nearest operator, NCB of Wem. I say nearest, they are still 16 miles away... and also, no longer exist as a separate entity having been purchased by Lakeside of Ellesmere in 2019. New to that long-standing Volvo operator Park's of Hamilton as 1 RWM (the second of seven Park's coaches to carry the plate), B15 NCB is seen on a rather dismal day on Weymouth seafront. (PG)

In 2006, FirstGroup unveiled 'The Future of Travel', or FTR – a rapid-transit bus system in York, Leeds, Luton Airport and Swansea using a fleet of thirty-nine Wright StreetCar-bodied B7LAs. The first withdrawals started after less than six years, and by 2016 all had been replaced. New to First York in 2006, First Leeds 19007 (YK06 ATY) is seen travelling up Eastgate en route to Bradford. (RS)

I know, I know… another major operator purchasing service buses second-hand from an independent! Anglian Bus of Beccles in Suffolk operated its first public bus service in 1999 and for a small independent operator purchased a healthy number of new buses each year until selling to the Go-Ahead Group in 2012. In 2006, five brand-new Wright Eclipse-bodied B7RLEs entered the fleet, including AU06 BPO, which was sold to Blackpool Transport in 2010. (RS)

Spanish bodybuilder Sunsundegui was founded in 1944 to repair railway carriages for the Spanish state railway company RENFE, building its first coach bodies in 1987 when RENFE took the repair work in-house. When Sunsundegui launched the Sideral body, they signed a deal with Volvo ensuring that all Sideral bodies would be fitted onto Volvo chassis. Tri-axle B12B OK06 AOL from the fleet of Abbott of Leeming is seen entering London Victoria coach station. (PG)

While most schools hire in coaches for pupil transport, Taunton School (notable alumni include Leslie Scott, who invented the game Jenga) operates full-size coaches on its own operator's licence, and all vehicles were purchased brand new. Van Hool Alizee T9-bodied B12B WA56 ENR was one of identical twins purchased in 2007 and is seen in Street waiting for its little darlings to return. (PG)

Thames Travel was founded as recently as 1998 with four buses and expanded by gaining subsidised contracts on behalf of Oxfordshire and Berkshire county councils, as well as filling the hole when long-established operators Tillingbourne and Chiltern Queens closed their doors. The Go-Ahead Group acquired Thames Travel in 2011, resulting in the transfer of five Wright Gemini-bodied B9TLs from Go-Ahead London. 934 (LX06 EAE), the former WVL243, is seen outside Didcot Parkway railway station. (PG)

The original South Wales Transport started operating buses around Swansea in 1914 and is nowadays named First Cymru, a FirstGroup subsidiary. In 2004, the SWT name was revived by a former director of First Cymru to run in competition with his former company, operating a network of services from a base in Llansamlet. Coaches also feature in the fleet, including this impressive 15-metre-long Plaxton Panther-bodied B12BT SV56 BWC, new to Stagecoach Bluebird for Megabus duties. (PG)

We've had *Goliath*, now we've got *Hamish*! In 2017 Lothian Transport chose Macmillan Cancer support as their charity of choice and had B9TL Wright Gemini 856 (SN57 DFJ) wrapped in this Kinloch Anderson tartan. The name 'Hamish' was chosen by the good people of Edinburgh, purportedly because 'he will get you near to your hame (home)'. It is seen on Edinburgh's Princes Street with the Scott Memorial in the background. (PG)

Carnforth-based The Travellers Choice can trace its origins as far back as 1872 when Robert Shaw commenced his horse-drawn cart business. In the mid-1970s, the operations of Hadwin of Ulverston were acquired, and for many years the company traded as Shaw-Hadwin. B12B Jonckheere JHV 3182 NF was new to Ellison's of St Helens as FJ08 FZH and is seen in Brighton. (PG)

As I commenced the research for this book it was announced that long-established Kenzies Coaches would be closing following the retirement of owner Cyril Kenzie. Whether it be one of their fleet of preserved coaches or one of the operational fleet, all were kept in immaculate condition. New to Kenzies in 2008 as YJ08 NSV was Van Hool-bodied B12B H2 CBK. It was seen in Brighton in 2014. (PG)

The delightful Derbyshire town of Ashbourne, the gateway to the Peak District, is home to Glovers coaches, whose current flagship is 9700-bodied B12BT AIG 8900. New in 2008 to Mangan of Gortahork, County Donegal-registered 08-DL-970, it came over the water in 2010 and joined Glovers in 2015. (RS)

One of the biggest rise and fall stories in recent years was Wessex Connect. Formed in 2007 when Rotala purchased South Gloucestershire Bus & Coach's bus operations, it grew to more than a hundred buses. Routes serving the University of the West of England carried over 6,000 students per day, growing from three routes needing five buses to eight routes needing twenty-six. Unfortunately, the loss of local authority-subsidised services was too much to bear, and operations ceased in September 2018. Seen in Bath is Plaxton Centro-bodied B7RLE 30502 (BX58 APF). (RS)

With the impressive backdrop of Breadsall Priory in Derbyshire, which has the distinction of being the oldest Marriott hotel in the world), we see Edwards of Eastbourne's JE09 LJE. Another Sunsundegui Sideral, but this time on a B7R, it was new to Doig's of Glasgow as FN09 AOD. (PG)

Megabus-liveried Plaxton Panther-bodied B12BT 54059 (KX 59 DLN) leaves Chesterfield on a rail replacement journey to Derby. It was new to Midland Red South in 2009 for use on Megabus duties but was transferred within Stagecoach to Yorkshire Traction (Stagecoach Yorkshire) to operate the long-term rail replacement contract. (RS)

These five B9s of Mortons Travel of Tadley in Hampshire might look identical, but one is slightly different from the rest. Four have Optare Olympus bodies; the odd man out is P1 KGF, fitted with an East Lancs Olympus body. The Olympus was launched by East Lancs in 2006 but the company went into administration less than a year later, with Optare taking over their designs in 2008. All are fitted with 100 coach seats, with PO59 KGF on the left new to Mortons. The other four were acquired second-hand from various sources. (PG)